ALL AROUND THE WORLD
ECUADOR

by Joanne Mattern

pogo

Ideas for Parents and Teachers

Pogo Books let children practice reading informational text while introducing them to nonfiction features such as headings, labels, sidebars, maps, and diagrams, as well as a table of contents, glossary, and index.

Carefully leveled text with a strong photo match offers early fluent readers the support they need to succeed.

Before Reading

- "Walk" through the book and point out the various nonfiction features. Ask the student what purpose each feature serves.
- Look at the glossary together. Read and discuss the words.

Read the Book

- Have the child read the book independently.
- Invite him or her to list questions that arise from reading.

After Reading

- Discuss the child's questions. Talk about how he or she might find answers to those questions.
- Prompt the child to think more. Ask: Interesting animals are found throughout Ecuador. What animals live near you?

Pogo Books are published by Jump!
5357 Penn Avenue South
Minneapolis, MN 55419
www.jumplibrary.com

Library of Congress Cataloging-in-Publication Data

Names: Mattern, Joanne, 1963- author.
Title: Ecuador / by Joanne Mattern.
Description: Pogo books. | Minneapolis, MN : Jump!, [2019]
Series: All around the world | Includes index.
Audience: Ages 7-10.
Identifiers: LCCN 2018014525 (print)
LCCN 2018015416 (ebook)
ISBN 9781641281485 (e-book)
ISBN 9781641281461 (hardcover : alk. paper)
ISBN 9781641281478 (pbk.)
Subjects: LCSH: Ecuador—Juvenile literature.
Classification: LCC F3708.5 (ebook)
LCC F3708.5 .M38 2019 (print) | DDC 986.6—dc23
LC record available at https://lccn.loc.gov/2018014525

Editor: Kristine Spanier
Designer: Molly Ballanger

Photo Credits: Ecuadorpostales/Shutterstock, cover, 16; Natursports/Shutterstock, 1; Pixfiction/Shutterstock, 3; Rusiana Iurchenko/Shutterstock, 4; Fotos593/Shutterstock, 5; rchphoto/iStock, 6-7; lunatv/iStock, 8-9; Diana Zuleta/Shutterstock,10; Matt Jacques/Alamy, 11; Robert Landau/Alamy, 12-13; Barna Tanko/Shutterstock, 14-15; Eugene Berman/Shutterstock, 17; Madlen/Shutterstock, 18l; Yai/Shutterstock, 18-19; Michael Nolan/robertharding/Superstock, 20-21tl; Roland Seitre/Minden Pictures/Superstock, 20-21bl; Andyd/Getty, 20-21tr; bukentagen/Shutterstock, 20-21br, YamabikaY/Shutterstock, 23.

Printed in the United States of America at Corporate Graphics in North Mankato, Minnesota.

TABLE OF CONTENTS

CHAPTER 1
Welcome to Ecuador! 4

CHAPTER 2
Life in Ecuador 10

CHAPTER 3
The Land and Animals 16

QUICK FACTS & TOOLS
At a Glance 22
Glossary 23
Index 24
To Learn More 24

CHAPTER 1

WELCOME TO ECUADOR!

Hola! That is how you say "hello" in Ecuador. It is a beautiful country in South America.

equator monument

Ecuador is on the **equator**. This is how the country got its name.

Let's explore!

People have lived in Ecuador for thousands of years. Early people were part of the Inca **Empire**. They wove bright **textiles**. Later, people came from Europe.

Peru and Spain ruled Ecuador for many years. In 1830, it became **independent**. People here continue the weaving tradition.

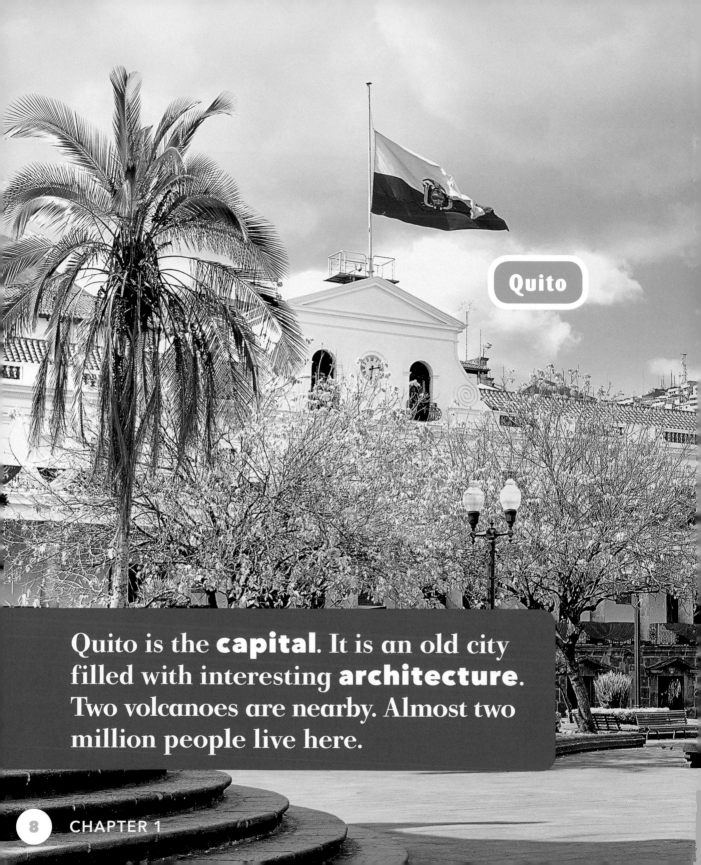

Quito

Quito is the **capital**. It is an old city filled with interesting **architecture**. Two volcanoes are nearby. Almost two million people live here.

TAKE A LOOK!

Each element of Ecuador's flag **symbolizes** an important value of the country's people.

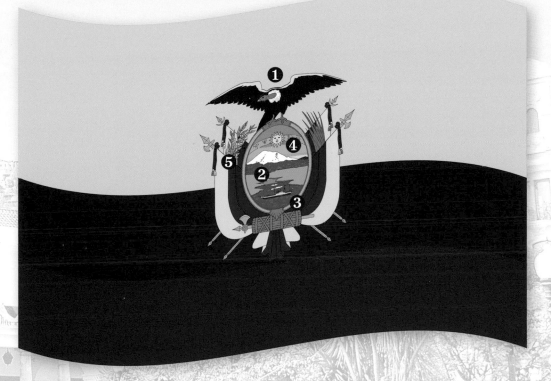

■ = rich crops
■ = sea and sky
■ = people who died in the battles for independence
❶ condor: shelter and protection
❷ mountain: uniting of the central highlands and the coast
❸ boat: trade
❹ sun: Incan history
❺ branches: victory in fight for independence

CHAPTER 2

LIFE IN ECUADOR

People in Ecuador enjoy many tasty foods. One is locro. It is a soup made with potatoes, cheese, and avocados. Chicken and rice are also favorite foods.

locro ·····▶

People here love to play sports! Soccer is the most popular. Basketball and volleyball are favorites, too.

Children here start school when they are six years old. Some students must walk up to three miles (4.8 kilometers) to get to school. Many leave school after the age of 14 to earn money.

DID YOU KNOW?

Some students in Ecuador take canoes to school. Others take donkeys. How do you get to school?

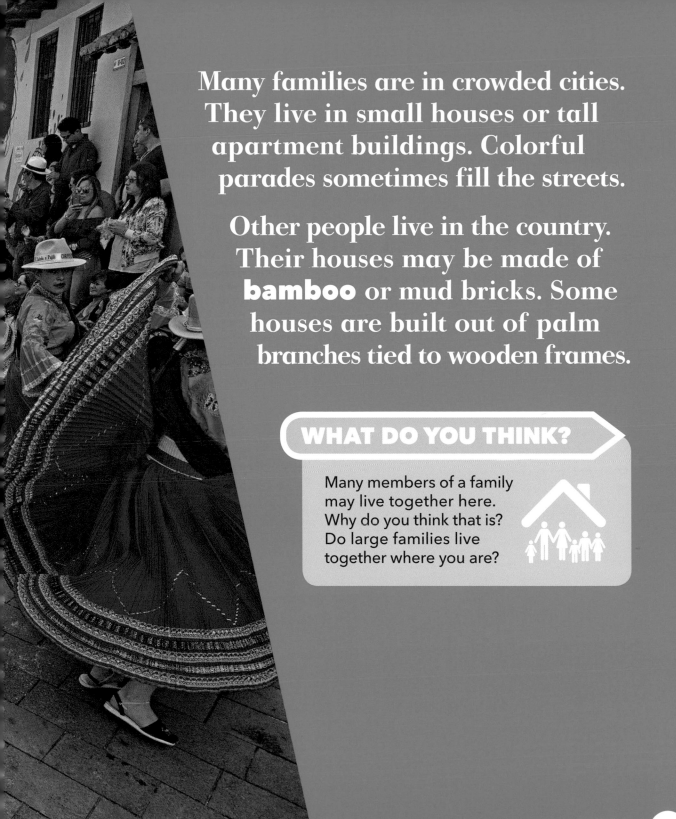

Many families are in crowded cities. They live in small houses or tall apartment buildings. Colorful parades sometimes fill the streets.

Other people live in the country. Their houses may be made of **bamboo** or mud bricks. Some houses are built out of palm branches tied to wooden frames.

WHAT DO YOU THINK?

Many members of a family may live together here. Why do you think that is? Do large families live together where you are?

CHAPTER 3

THE LAND AND ANIMALS

Many different landscapes are here. Mountains are in the middle of the country. The Andes are the highest mountains here.

Andes

The Pacific Coast is low and flat. **Wetlands** are in the north. The land in the south is hot and dry. The Amazon **Rain Forest** is in the east.

Amazon
Rain Forest

The warm **climate** is good for growing **crops**. Roses grow here. So do bananas and coffee plants. Cacao beans are grown to make cocoa powder. These crops are **exported** all around the world.

◀ · · · · · **cocoa powder**

cacao
beans

cacao pod

sloth

spectacled bear

tapir

condor

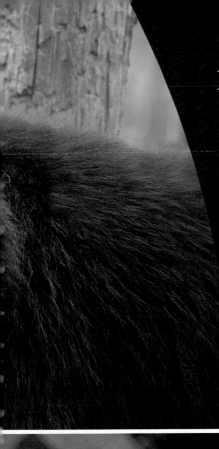

Many animals call Ecuador home. Monkeys live in the rain forest. Sloths hang from branches. Tapirs roam around. Spectacled bears live in the mountains. So do huge condors.

Ecuador is full of color and life! What a beautiful place to visit!

WHAT DO YOU THINK?

The Galápagos Islands are part of Ecuador. Some animals on the islands do not live anywhere else. An example is the marine iguana. And the Galápagos fur seal. Why do you think this is?

QUICK FACTS & TOOLS

Pacific Ocean • COLUMBIA • ECUADOR • Quito★ • Andes • Equator • Amazon Rain Forest • GALÁPAGOS ISLANDS • PERU • N W E S

ECUADOR

Location: South America

Size: 109,484 square miles (283,561 square kilometers)

Population: 16,290,913 (July 2017 estimate)

Capital: Quito

Type of Government: presidential republic

Languages: Spanish and Quechua

Exports: petroleum, bananas, flowers, cacao, coffee, wood, fish

Currency: U.S. dollar

architecture: A style of building.

bamboo: A woody grass that grows in warm places.

capital: A city where government leaders meet.

climate: The weather typical of a certain place over a long period of time.

crops: Plants grown for food.

empire: A group of countries or states that has the same ruler.

equator: An imaginary line around the center of the Earth.

exported: Sold to other countries.

independent: Free from a controlling authority.

rain forest: A thick, tropical forest.

revenue: Income produced by a given source.

symbolizes: Represents a concept or an idea.

textiles: Woven or knitted fabrics or cloths.

wetlands: Land where there is a lot of moisture in the soil.

Ecuador's currency

INDEX

Amazon Rain Forest 17, 21

Andes 16

animals 21

architecture 8

capital 8

climate 18

crops 18

equator 5

Europe 7

flag 9

foods 10

Galápagos Islands 21

Inca Empire 7

independence 7, 9

Pacific Coast 17

parades 15

Peru 7

Quito 8

school 12

South America 4

Spain 7

sports 11

textiles 7

volcanoes 8

TO LEARN MORE

Learning more is as easy as 1, 2, 3.

1) Go to www.factsurfer.com

2) Enter "Ecuador" into the search box.

3) Click the "Surf" button to see a list of websites.

With factsurfer, finding more information is just a click away.